**T** his book includes 5 games that help your children or students **l** earn and remember musical notes, their location on the staff and on the keyboard:

**G** ame #1 **Do-Re-Mi Dominos.** Note names and symbols are taught by the correspondence between the notes (Do, Re, Mi, Fa, etc.) and their location on the musical staff.

**G** ame #2 **CDEF Dominos** teaches the correspondence between note letter notations (C, D, E, F, etc.) and their locations on the musical staff.

**G** ame #3 **Find a Pair Card Game**. There are two sets of cards, one with note staff location and the other with note keyboard location. Cards need to be matched appropriately. The correct choice can be confirmed with the note name, which is on the reverse of all cards.

**G** ame #4 **Treble Clef Dominos** teaches the correspondence between treble clef notes and their place on the keyboard.

**G** ame #5 **Bass Clef Dominos** teaches the correspondence between bass clef notes and their place on the keyboard.

Cut out the cards for each game from the book. Storage them separately in little plastic baggies, laminate for maximum durability.

**Dominos rules:**
Play individually or in pairs. Layout dominoes face down and shuffle. Each player takes 7 dominoes. Player 1 lays down any domino. Next to it, player 2 lays a domino which is its counterpart. Make sure the two joined dominoes represent the same musical note.

If you do not have a domino to match, pick one from the pile. Whoever plays all dominoes first wins. The game also ends when there are no more possibilities. When playing alone, try to connect all dominoes.

These games are ideal for use at a music school or as a home activity.

# Game #3

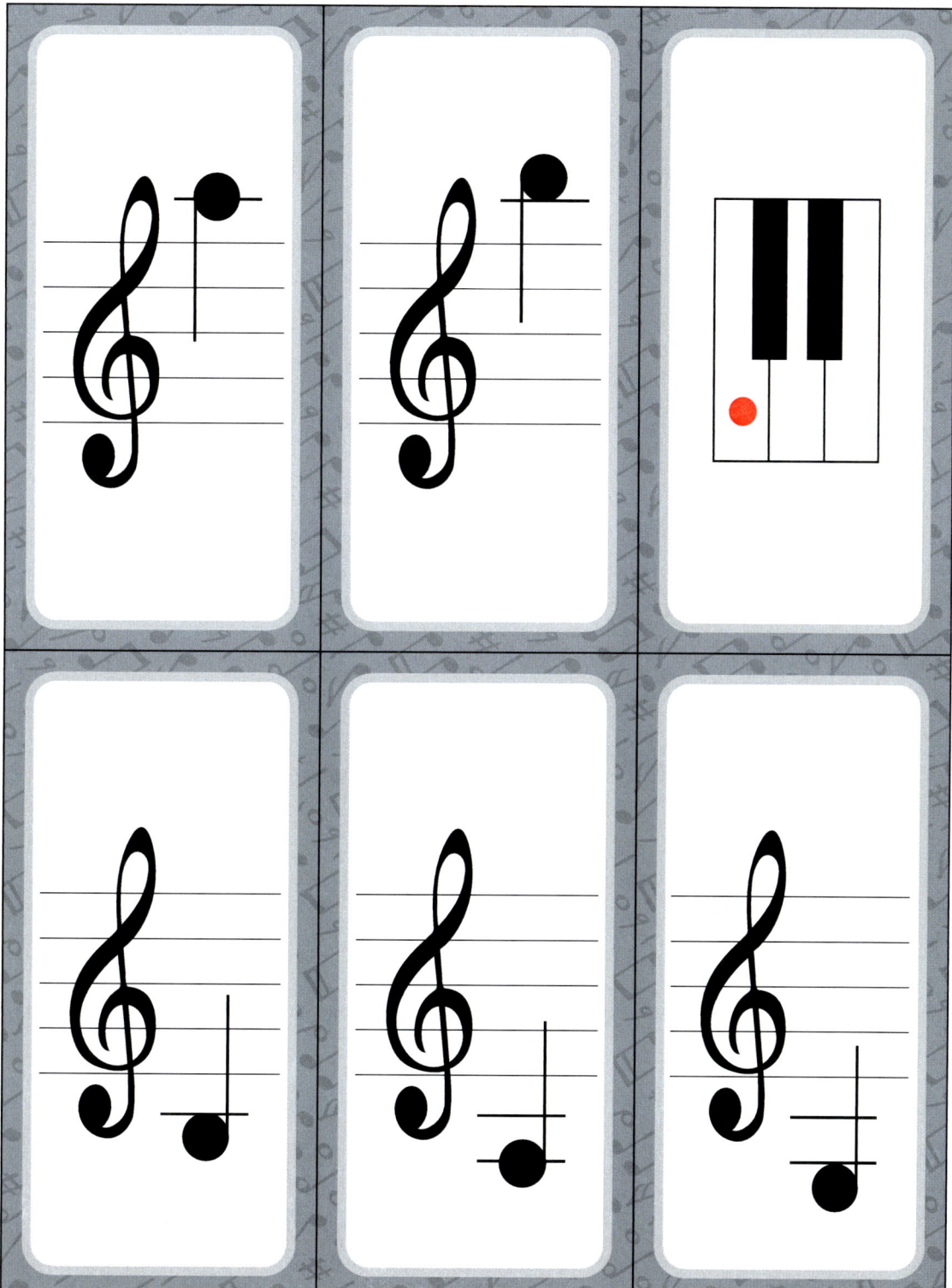

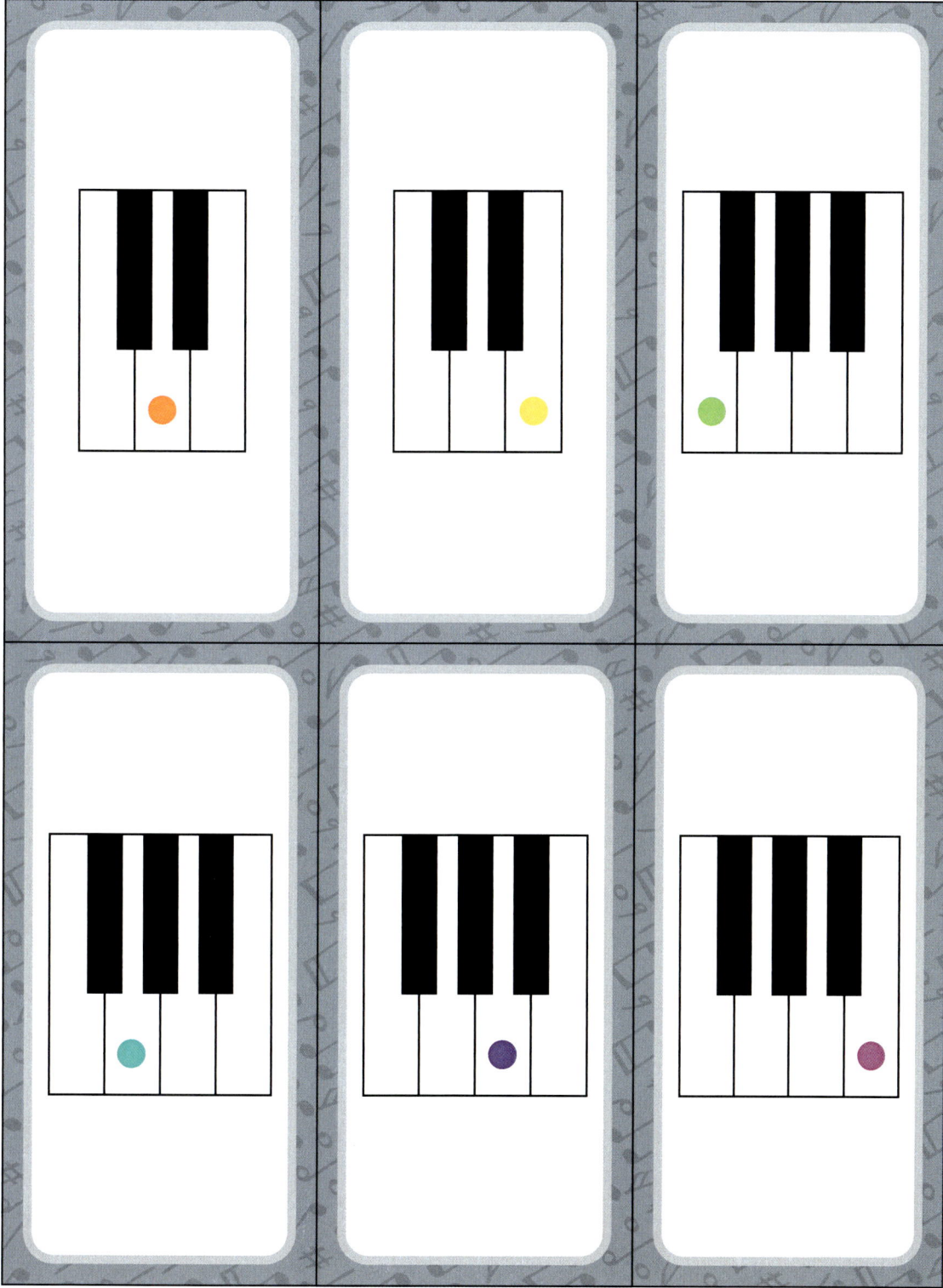

# Game # 4

# Game #5

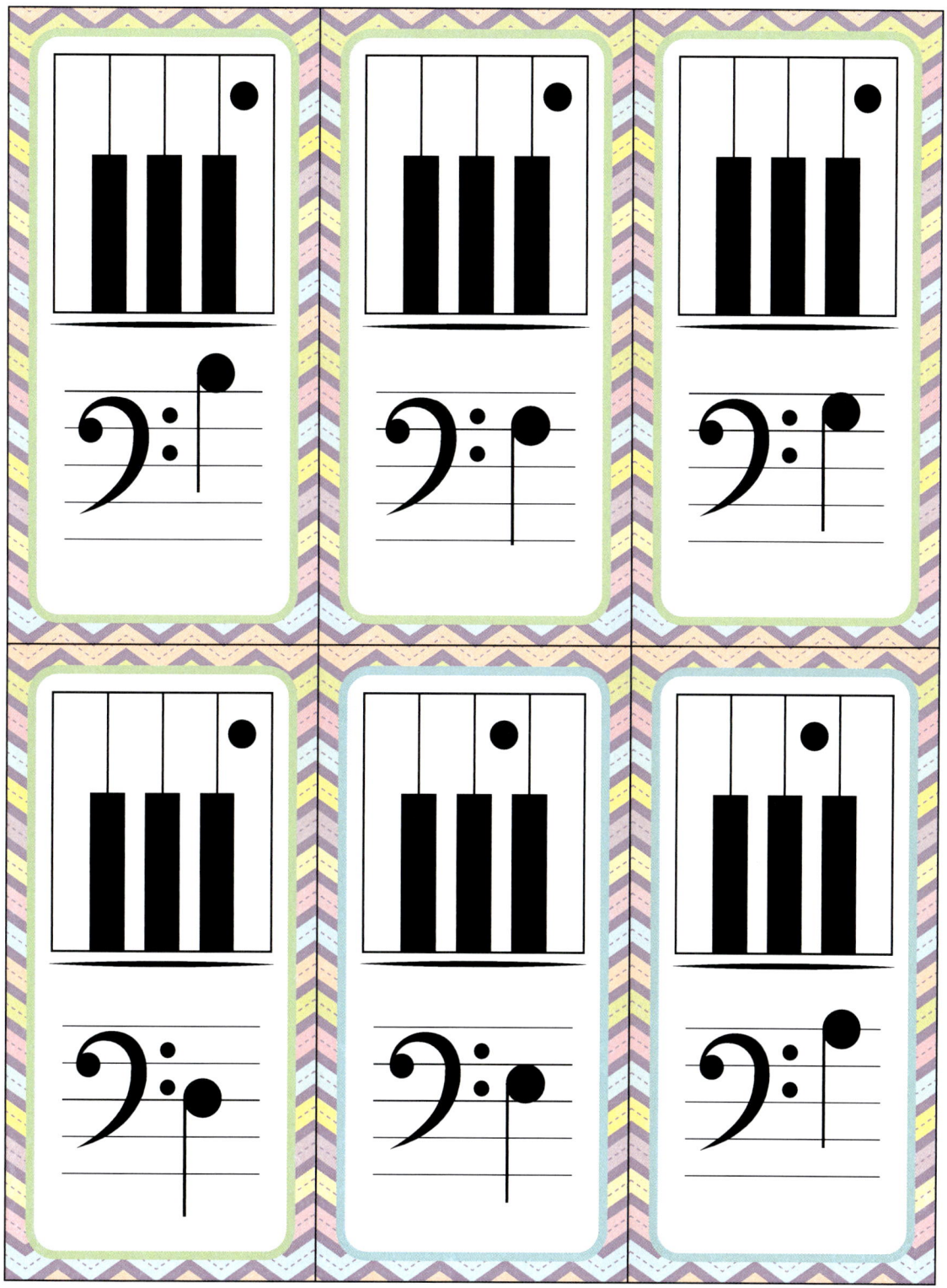

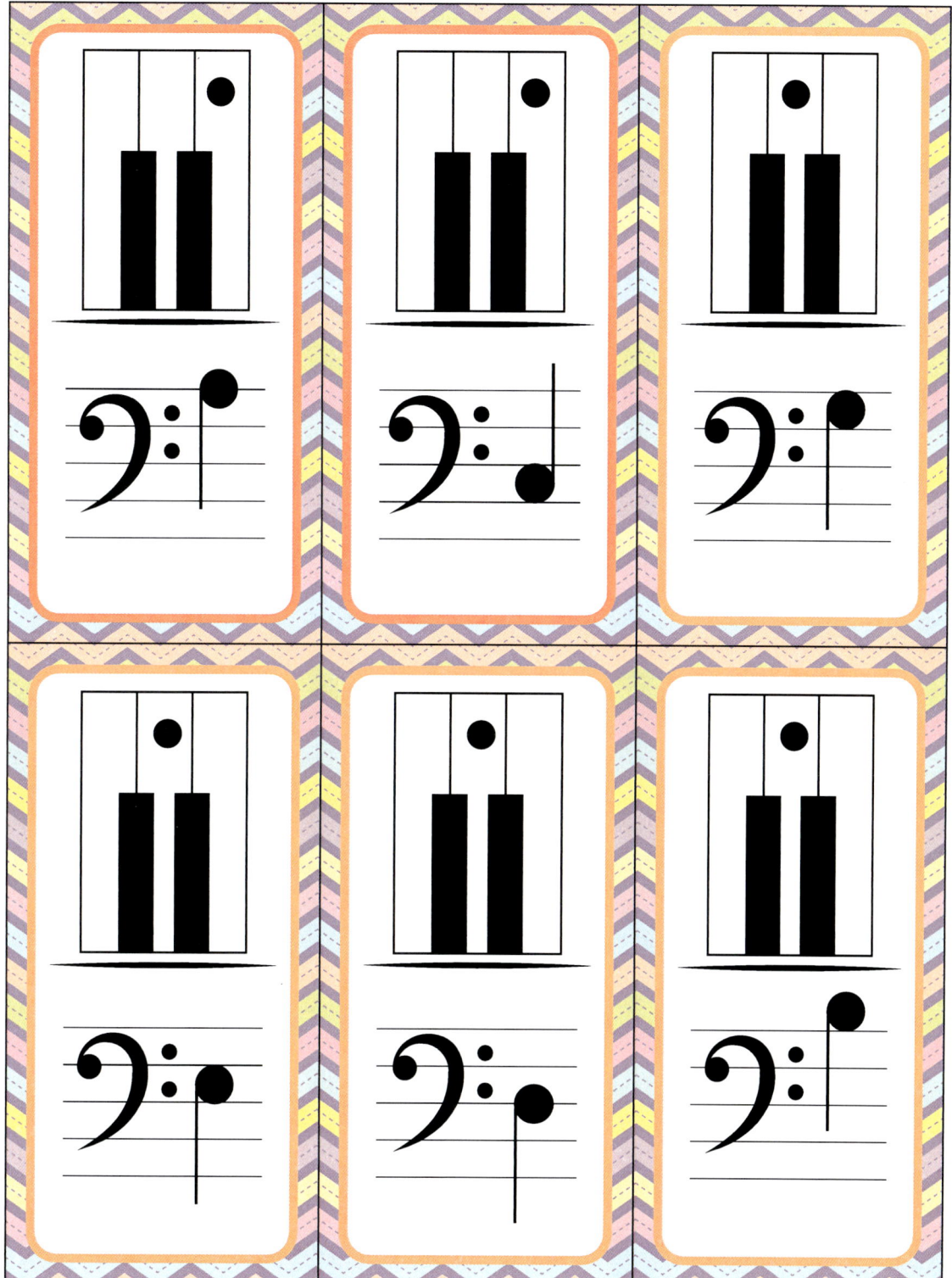

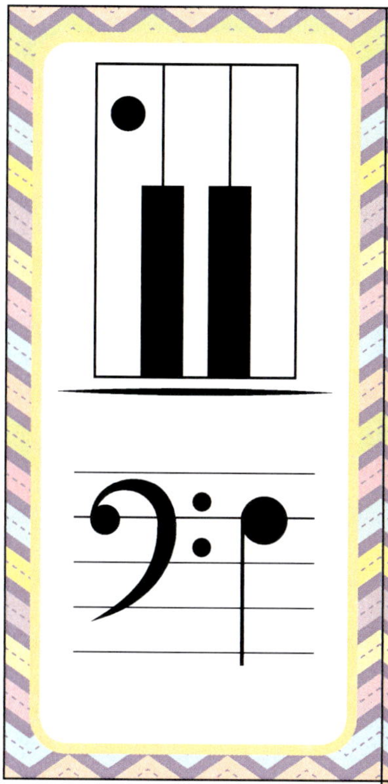